Where do people live?

W9-BYI-792

130

In houses small

or grand.

Some homes are in the city,

and some have
trees and land.

Homes are built of many things—

wood, straw, stone, and clay.

And houses come in many shades.

Find the purple, white, and gray.

Which home has no windows, and which is made of glass?

Which one has a roof of mud, and which a roof of grass?

Which home is on a mountaintop? Which is near the ocean?

Which homes are built to stay in place?
Which are made for motion?

Some houses stand in tidy rows, as cozy as can be.

And others have no neighbors,
as far as the eye can see.

You've seen some homes and places
and there are many more.
What kinds of homes do you see
when you open up your door?